T0012112

THE LITTLE BOOK OF
NATIONAL PARKS

Published in 2022 by OH!
An Imprint of Welbeck Non-Fiction Limited,
part of Welbeck Publishing Group.
Based in London and Sydney.
www.welbeckpublishing.com

Disclaimer:
This book is intended for general informational purposes only and should not be relied upon as recommending or promoting any specific practice, diet or method of treatment. It is not intended to diagnose, advise, treat or prevent any illness or condition and is not a substitute for advice from a professional practitioner of the subject matter contained in this book. You should not use the information in this book as a substitute for medication, nutritional, diet, spiritual or other treatment that is prescribed by your practitioner. The publisher makes no representations or warranties with respect to the accuracy, completeness or currency of the contents of this work, and specifically disclaim, without limitation, any implied warranties of merchantability or fitness for a particular purpose and any injury, illness, damage, death, liability or loss incurred, directly or indirectly from the use or application of any of the contents of this book. Furthermore, the publisher is not affiliated with and does not sponsor or endorse any uses of or beliefs about in any way referred in this book.

ISBN 978-1-80069-171-1

Compiled and written by: Lisa Dyer
Editorial: Vicroria Godden
Project manager: Russell Porter
Design: Tony Seddon
Production: Rachel Burgess

A CIP catalogue record for this book is available from the British Library

Printed in China

10 9 8 7 6 5 4 3 2 1

Illustrations: Freepik.com

THE LITTLE BOOK OF
NATIONAL
PARKS

DRAMATIC LANDSCAPES AND
NATURAL WONDERS OF THE USA

CONTENTS

INTRODUCTION

From sea to shining sea, America is host to some of the most dramatic landscapes on earth. Whether you are a camper or a climber, a sightseer or a thrill-seeker, you will find spectacular sights in the nation's parks, from the tallest trees of the Redwood, the desert of Death Valley, and the gorge of the Grand Canyon to the snowy mountains of Mount Rainier and the jagged peaks of the Grand Teton.

On the following pages you can take a virtual tour of every park—cave and crag, gorge and glacier—exploring their geographical features, wildlife, and biodiversity. You can revisit the lands as they were first seen by Native Americans and the early explorers, pioneers, and homesteaders who settled the frontiers or revel in the majesty of nature that is more immense and profound than you can imagine.

In the first chapter, Wilderness Protected, you will discover the beginnings of the park service and get an idea of a small sampling of the wide variety of excursions and activities the parks offer. There are tips here for visiting and hiking and ways you can help preserve and protect these remarkable national treasures.

The remaining chapters are organized by region, and states within those regions, so you can discover the highlights of each of the national parks. There are so many ways to immerse yourself in the natural surroundings, from fishing and hiking to white-water rafting and mountain climbing. There are family-friendly places with easy hour-long trails and remote locations for only the most extreme adventurers. There are summits to scale and underwater wonderworlds to behold.

For more information, visit the national parks website, www.nps.gov, where you can discover everything you need to know to plan a visit.

CHAPTER
ONE

Wilderness Protected

Find out why the national parks were established, what they protect, and how you can enjoy and explore them.

"

National parks are the best idea we ever had. Absolutely American, absolutely democratic, they reflect us at our best rather than our worst.

"

Wallace Stegner, novelist and environmentalist, *Wilderness* **magazine, 1983**

Credit for the concept of the national parks is given to the artist George Catlin, who in 1832 traveled the northern Great Plains where he became concerned about the destruction of Native American civilization, wildlife, and wilderness. The idea was promoted by various politicians, conservationists, and campaigners, but it wasn't until President Theodore Roosevelt signed the Antiquities Act in 1906 that the beginnings of a federal program were established.

It was 44 years after President Ulysses S. Grant established Yellowstone as a protected park in 1872 that President Woodrow Wilson created the National Park Service to protect and maintain the nation's wilderness regions, on August 25, 1916. It is a bureau of the U.S. Department of the Interior.

President Franklin D. Roosevelt's New Deal helped bring in a program of natural resource conservation. The Civilian Conservation Corps (CCC) was formed in 1933 for unemployed young male volunteers, a work-study program to improve and maintain the national resources and rural environments, including the federal parks, but also state and local lands.

The national parks preserve
nationally and globally
significant scenic areas and
nature reserves. Of the 63 parks,
13 are UNESCO World Heritage
sites and many are part of larger
biosphere reserves. In addition
to the parks, the National
Park Service protects shores,
parkways, preserves, historical
sites, monuments, battlefields,
and military parks.

In addition to preserving natural resources, wildlife habitats, and ecosystems, protecting clean water and clean air, the parks provide open wilderness space and recreation for current and future generations. Whether you enjoy rock or ice climbing, hiking, cycling, kayaking, camping, orienteering, skiing, fishing, or watersports, there are adventures for everyone, from the birdwatcher to the explorer.

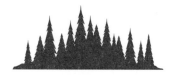

"

Everybody needs beauty
as well as bread, places
to play in and pray in,
where nature may heal
and give strength to
body and soul.

"

John Muir, *The Yosemite* (1912)

The parks have clear trails and recommended routes for different levels, such as easy, moderate, and strenuous hikes.

There are backcountry trails for independent backtrackers as well as ranger-led tours. There are hikes across glaciers and rainforests, through gorge and underground, along shorelines and on boardwalks in forests.

HIKING TIPS

Research your trip thoroughly, check the weather before you go, and don't rely on cellular service or a reliable water supply. Always check the National Parks website: www.nps.gov

❧ Wear sturdy and comfortable footwear and be prepared for weather changes.

❧ Take plenty of snacks and water.

❧ Take a flashlight, compass, and map. You may not be able to rely on GPS or phone signals.

❧ Check in with the park ranger before leaving and heed any warnings.

❧ Know your physical limits.

❧ Stay on designated trails for your safety and also to prevent erosion and damage to vegetation.

❧ Respect and stay clear of the wildlife. This is their natural habitat and they will behave accordingly.

❧ Follow the countryside code: Don't litter and leave no trace behind.

FIVE POPULAR HIKES

🐾 The Mist Trail in Yosemite is 3 miles (4.8 km) and the mist from the waterfalls and river can drench hikers; alternatively climbers seeking heights should try the Half Dome.

🐾 The Skyline Trail in Mount Rainier is a 6-mile (9.6-km) hike through falls, forest, and snow-capped mountain.

🐾 The Navajo Loop in Bryce Canyon is a short 2-mile (3.2-km) family-friendly hike with dramatic views, like the Thor's Hammer hoodoo.

🐾 The mostly paved Rim Trail in the Grand Canyon is 13 miles (21 km) and there's a shuttlebus you can hop on and off.

🐾 The Narrows in Zion, a gorge with walls 1,000 feet (305 m) high. You'll have to wade through the Virgin River and you can take the shorter upstream route or a 16-mile (9.6-km) route through Chamberlain's Ranch, which requires a permit.

66

Within National Parks is
room—glorious room—room
in which to find ourselves,
in which to think and hope,
to dream and plan, to rest
and resolve.

99

Enos Mills, *Your National Parks* (1917)

66

If future generations are to remember us with gratitude rather than contempt, we must leave them something more than the miracles of technology. We must leave them a glimpse of the world as it was in the beginning, not just after we got through it.

99

President Lyndon B. Johnson, on signing the Wilderness Act, September 3, 1964

The parks services work
with heritage, educational, and
historian organizations,
businesses and nonprofits,
and local communities and
indigenous tribes, to conserve
and celebrate natural
history and traditions as well
as the environment.

With climate change and
human development, there is increased
recognition of the parks' fragility.

Two of the most ecologically sensitive,
Zion and Denali, ban cars and transport
visitors by bus, as does Yellowstone.
Interactions of humans with the animal
life is also discouraged. But climate
change is the biggest threat, shrinking
ice caps and glaciers, affecting animal
habitats and endangering species,
such as the bighorn sheep and American
pika (boulder bunny).

SUSTAINABLE PRACTICES

There are simple ways each person can help with conservation and contribute to the health and sustainability of national parks. Adopt practices such as:

🌲 Reducing your carbon footprint

🌲 Reduce, reuse, and recycle

🌲 Eat and buy locally

🌲 Conserve water and energy

🌲 Get outdoors! Walk or cycle rather than drive whenever possible.

CHAPTER
TWO

Alaska

This state features the four largest parks and the most remote and untouched wilderness in the country, where dark winters are lit by the aurora borealis and summers are alive with wildlife and greenery.

DENALI
Denali Borough, Alaska

Six million acres of wilderness bisected by one 92-mile (150-km) ribbon road, and home to Denali (formerly Mount Kinley), North America's tallest peak at 20,310 feet (6,190 meters), the park is a destination for mountaineering, skiing, and adventuring.

According to legend, Yahoo, an Alaskan possessed of power but without a wife, took the daughter of the raven chief. The chief pursued him, causing a storm that threatened to capsize his canoe, but Yahoo turned the waves into mountains of stone just in time—a smaller one, Foraker, and one he named Denali, meaning "the great one."

GATES OF THE ARCTIC
Bettles, Alaska

The least visited national park and the most remote, without roads, trails, or services and with unpredictable weather, the park is located completely north of the Arctic Circle and encompasses the central Brooks Range mountains. Hiding within the layers of rock are fossils as old as 400 million years!

A true wilderness of
8.4 million acres,
the park is virtually unchanged
except by the forces of nature.
Avoid winter when the
average temperature is
-67°F (-55°C)
amid constant darkness.

For more than 11,000 years, there has been an unbroken physical and spiritual link between the native Nunamiut who live here and the caribou they hunt.

The Nunamiut devised complex hunting rituals, such as the use of human-like stone figures (iñuksuit) to help direct caribou over many miles into corrals, lakes, or rivers where hunters waited with spears or bows and arrows.

66

Caribou meat is our meat since I was born. I was raised with it. The skin was my clothes. The meat was my diet and the broth was my drink… Without caribou meat, what would I eat…?

99

Rachel Riley, Nunamiut elder, nps.gov

GLACIER BAY
Gustavus, Alaska

From sea to summit, the park covers rugged mountains, dynamic glaciers, rainforest, coastlines, and fjords with tides that swell as much as 20 vertical feet. Since its exploration by John Muir in 1879, scientists from around the world have come to explore its pristine ecosystems.

The spiritual homeland of
the Huna Tlingit people, the bay
was known as *s'e shuyee* or "the
edge of the glacial silt" and was
habitable for many centuries until
about 300 years ago when glacier
surges forced the Tlingit out.

Once the ice retreated, the place
became known as *sit' eeti gheeyi*,
"the bay in place of the glacier."

KATMAI
King Salmon, Alaska

The park was established in 1918
to protect the region devasted by the
Novarupta volcano on June 6, 1912,
one of the five largest eruptions in
recorded history.

Mount Katmai collapsed, ash soared
to over 100,000 feet (32 km) into
the atmosphere, and nearby Kodiak
Island was plunged into a darkness that
lasted three days.

The ash cloud eventually encircled
the earth. To date, no eruption has
surpassed it.

The Valley of Ten Thousand
Smokes was the name given
by Robert F. Griggs from the
National Geographic Society to
the remains of the Novarupta
volcano, to describe the
thousands of fumaroles that
vented steam from the ash
on the valley floor.

KENAI FJORDS
Seward, Alaska

The Ice Age lingers here with nearly 40 glaciers flowing from the Harding Icefield.

Take a hike to see horizons of ice and snow interrupted by the occasional *nunatak* (peaks), but as there is approximately 1,000 feet (305 meters) of elevation per mile, allow an hour per mile for walking.

❝

To the lover of pure wildness
Alaska is one of the most
wonderful countries in the
world… it seems as if surely
we must at length reach the
very paradise of the poets, the
abode of the blessed.

❞

John Muir, *Travels in Alaska* (1915)

KOBUK VALLEY
Kotzebue, Alaska

Half a million caribou migrate through 25 miles (40 km) of sculpted sand dunes here—the largest dune complex in the Arctic with some ridges over 200 feet (61 meters) tall.

The park is home to 162 bird species, including the tundra swan, Arctic tern, northern goshawk, and harlequin duck, while the Kobuk River is one of the few places in the world where sheefish (*Stenodus leucichthys*), often exceeding 4 feet (1.2 meters) in length, can be found.

LAKE CLARK
Port Alsworth, Alaska

Four million acres of volcanic
and glacier landscape is dotted
with iridescent and turquoise
blue lakes, including the
40-mile (64-km)-long Lake
Clark, known to the Dena'ina
people as *Qizhjeh Vena*, "the lake
where people gathered."

Glass beads were once important trade items to the native Athabascan villagers, first co-existing with porcupine quillwork and then replacing it. More than 1,200 glass trade beads, from Venetian to Russian in origin, have been discovered in Kijik, an abandoned town on the shores of the lake.

An icon of wilderness self-sufficiency, Richard Proenneke constructed a cabin on the Twin Lakes in the park in the 1960s, using hand tools he built himself, and lived there alone for 30 years.

His journals and self-made film clips served as the inspiration for the documentary *Alone in the Wilderness* (2004). His cabin can be visited today.

66

I have found that some of the
simplest things have given me
the most pleasure... Did you ever
pick very large blueberries after
a summer rain, walk through a
grove of cottonwoods...
Come in out of the subzero and
shiver yourself warm in front
of a wood fire? The world is full
of such things.

99

Richard Proenneke, nps.gov

WRANGELL–ST. ELIAS
Copper Center, Alaska

The largest of the national parks rises from the ocean all the way up to 18,008 feet (5,490 meters).

At over

13.2 million acres,

the park is the same size as Yellowstone, Yosemite, and Switzerland combined!

Overwhelmingly vast, with peak after peak and glacier after glacier, there are four major mountain ranges—Wrangell, St. Elias, Chugach, and part of the Alaskan Range, which include nine of the 16 highest peaks in the U.S.

CHAPTER
THREE

The Pacific West

The Pacific states are host to a wide variety of climates and landscapes, from rainforest in Washington to the deserts of California and volcanic islands of Hawaii.

AMERICAN SAMOA
American Samoa

The only National Park Service site south of the Equator, American Samoa consists of expansive tropical rainforests on steep volcanic mountain slopes, surrounded by beautiful coral reefs, on three islands: Tutuila, Ofu, and Taʻ ū.

The oldest Polynesian culture, the Samoan way (*Fa'asamoa*) has specific rules on conduct. Each evening, around dusk, villagers observe prayers called *Sa*.

You must not sit with the legs stretched out and uncovered. And if asked to share *ava* (a local drink made from the root of the pepper plant), it is a great honor, so spill a few drops on the ground in front of you, then raise your cup and say *manuia* (mahn-WE-ah) before drinking.

CHANNEL ISLANDS
Ventura, California

The five islands—Anacapa, Santa Cruz, Santa Rosa, San Miguel, and Santa Barbara—are home to over 2,000 plant and animal species, of which 145 are found nowhere else in the world.

A subspecies of Torrey pine, considered one of the rarest pines in the world, is the last enduring member of a once widespread Pleistocene forest on Santa Rosa.

Pygmy mammoths,
only 4—6 feet
(1.2–1.8 meters) high,
once roamed
the island grasslands
and forests.

DEATH VALLEY
Death Valley, California & Nevada

A land of extremes and one
of the hottest places on earth,
the highest temperature
ever officially recorded,
according to the WMO (World
Meteorological Organization), is

134°F (56.7°C)

at Greenland Ranch,
Death Valley, on July 10, 1913.

More than 100 ghost towns and mining camps lie deserted in the park, remnants of the Gold Rush during 1849 and gold, silver, copper, and borax mining around 1900–19.

Rhyolite was the largest; in its heyday it had 50 saloons, 8 doctors, a stock exchange, and an opera house.

JOSHUA TREE
Twentynine Palms, California

Characterized by twisted, bristled Joshua Trees (actually a yucca plant) and rock formations dating back 1.7 billion years, the park straddles two distinct desert ecosystems: the cactus-dotted Colorado Desert and the Mojave Desert.

The local Cahuilla refer to
the trees as *hunuvat chiy'a* or
humwichawa, but it is said
that Mormon pioneers
named the tree, seeing in it
the outstretched arms of the
biblical Joshua leading the way
to Canaan, and thus guiding
them westward.

The park's naturally dark skies, elevation, and dry air make it well-known for stargazing while rock formations such as Skull Rock and the giant monolith known as the Great Burrito make it popular for climbing.

"

What draws us into the desert is the search for something intimate in the remote.

"

Edward Abbey, *Desert Solitaire* (1968)

LASSEN VOLCANIC
Mineral, California

Lassen has been volcanically active for about 3 million years and it is one of the few places in the world where all four types of volcano can be found: the plug dome, shield, cinder cone, and strato.

Watch out for the boiling springs! Many people have been burned badly by the acidic water lying under the thin crust of soil at such hydrothermal areas as Bumpass Hell, Sulphur Works, and Devils Kitchen.

PINNACLES
Paicines, California

Next to the San Andreas Fault and formed from plate changes, erosion, and the now-extinct Neenach volcano, the park contains the underworld mazes of the Ice-Age Talus caves, such as Bear Gulch and the Balconies. No spelunking skills are needed.

The Pinnacles homes
400 species of bees
over 42 square miles
(109 sq km) of land, the biggest
concentration anywhere
in the world.

REDWOOD
Del Norte and Humboldt counties, California

Descendants of the many Native Americans continue to live on and off reservations in the Redwood region.

Traditionally their homes were constructed of planks split from fallen redwoods, which were believed to be the bodies of Spirit Beings, a divine race who teach people the correct way to live.

Among the oldest and tallest
trees on earth, the first redwoods
appeared over 240 million years
ago. California's coast redwood
(*Sequoia sempervirens*) grow to a
height of 367 feet (112 meters) and
have a width of 22 feet (7 meters)
at the base.

The park's Hyperion is
thought to be the tallest living
redwood at
379 feet (116 meters).

Very rare ghost or albino redwood trees are scattered about the region. Lacking in chlorophyll, they are white in color and the needles are limp and waxy.

They remove noxious heavy metals from the soil and receive nourishment via the root system from healthier coast redwoods.

66

A grove of giant redwood or sequoias should be kept just as we keep a great and beautiful cathedral.

99

President Theodore Roosevelt,
A Book-Lover's Holidays in the Open (1916)

SEQUOIA & KINGS CANYON

Sierra Nevada, Tulare, and Fresno counties, California

The two conjoined parks are often referred to as the Land of Giants, as the dramatic, larger-than-life landscape features deep canyons, vast caverns, massive mountains, and some of the world's largest trees.

The General Sherman tree is
the largest by volume, at
**52,508 cubic feet
(1,487 cubic meters).**

It grows in Sequoia's Giant
Forest, which contains
five of the ten largest trees in
the world.

Giant Sequoias can live to
3,400 years old and are adapted
to periodic fire: their distinctive
reddish-brown bark is
18 inches (46 cm)
thick, extremely fibrous,
and fire-resistant.

Sequoia cones retain their seeds
for as long as 20 years, opening
up when dried out by fire and
dispensing their seeds onto the
bare fire-scorched soil.

The seeds are the size of a grain
of oatmeal—91,000 sequoia
seeds weigh just one pound!

YOSEMITE
Sierra Nevada, California

Three of the ten highest waterfalls in the world are located in Yosemite National Park, with Ribbon Falls nine times taller than Niagara Falls. Horsetail Fall, off the east side of El Capitan, is famous for appearing to be on fire when it reflects the orange glow of sunset.

Mariposa Grove is the largest sequoia grove in Yosemite and home to over 500 mature giants. In 1864 President Lincoln signed landmark legislation protecting the Mariposa Grove and Yosemite Valley for "public use, resort, and recreation" and marked the first time the federal government set aside scenic natural areas for conservation.

66

When I was about fifteen,
I went to work at Yosemite
National Park. It changed me
forever. Nature had carved
its own sculpture, and
I was part of it, not the other
way around.

99

Robert Redford, conservation.org

Lunar rainbows, or moonbows, can sometimes be seen in the park in spring and summer if the sky is clear and the moon is full. The moonlight creates a rainbow from the waterfall's mist.

GREAT BASIN
Baker, Nevada

The Great Basin bristlecone pines are extremely rare and grow in a twisted fashion at high altitude under harsh conditions.

Here lie the remains of the Prometheus tree, a Great Basin bristlecone, once recorded as the oldest tree in the world, estimated between 4,700–5,000 years old.

Visit the intricate caverns
and rare shield formations
of the Lehman caves, which
began forming as long as
5 million years ago, or go to
the Pictograph cave to see rock
art carved and painted by the
Fremont peoples, who inhabited
the area from about 1000
to 1300 CE.

HALEAKALĀ
Maui, Hawaii

The park is named after its dormant volcano, Haleakalā, which translates to "house of the sun." One of the Hawaiian *moʻolelo* (stories) tells how the demigod Māui ensnared the sun by tying it to a wiliwili tree to slow its path across the sky, so that his mother Hina might have enough time to dry her *kapa*, the bark-cloth that served as garments and bedding.

The only native mammals in Haleakalā are bats and seals. All other land mammals were brought by humans.

There are at least 1,000 native species of flowering plant, and 90% of these are found only in Hawaii.

HAWAI'I VOLCANOES
Hilo, Hawaii

Encompassing the summits of two of the world's most active volcanoes, Kīlauea and Mauna Loa, the park hosts the Volcano House hotel, where the occasional eruptive activity and lava can be seen up close. From 2008 to 2018, and again in 2020, visitors were able to view the orange light of a lava lake within the Halemaʻumaʻu crater from the dining room.

Located in Pānau Nui
on the southern flank of
Kīlauea volcano, Puʻuloa is
an archaeological site that
contains over
23,000 petroglyph images,
including geometric
and cryptic designs, human
figures, canoe sails, and
even feathered cape motifs.

CRATER LAKE
Cascade Mountains, Oregon

Previously known as Blue Lake and Lake Majesty, the deep blue lake sits in a caldera formed around 7,700 years ago from the collapse of the Mount Mazama volcano.

Fed by rain and snow and sometimes hidden in clouds, it is the deepest lake in the U.S. and one of the most pristine on earth.

In the oral history of the
Klamath tribe, the volcanic
eruption is told as a battle
between the sky god Skell and
the god of the underworld Llao.

Considered the home of the
Great Spirit, vision quests are
often held at the lake.

MOUNT RAINIER
Ashford, Enumclaw, Packwood, and Wilkeson, Washington

Originally called Tacoma or Tahoma, which means "the source of nourishment from the many streams coming from the slopes," Mount Rainier has 25 glaciers, the most of any mountain in the U.S., which provide the water source for six rivers: the Carbon, Cowlitz, Puyallup, Mowich, and Nisqually.

Named by Captain George Vancouver in 1792 after his friend Peter Rainier, a navy officer in the Revolutionary War, it is a relatively young volcano, at only about 500,000 years old, but overlooks the Cascade Range, which is at least 12 million years old.

NORTH CASCADES
Marblemount, Washington

The gateway to the national park, linking the Cascade mountains to the wilderness interior of the state, is a village called Stehekin, from a Salishan word meaning "the way through."

There are no access roads—you must make your way here by boat, plane, or on foot.

Fur traders were the first
to venture into the North
Cascades wilderness in the
late 1700s, looking for beaver,
bear, cougar, wolf, lynx, fisher,
marten, and fox to trap.

Three lookouts on the Cascades housed prominent Beat Generation writers: Gary Snyder manned the lookout on Crater Mountain in 1952 and on Sourdough Mountain in 1953; Philip Whalen lived on Sourdough; Jack Kerouac spent the summer of 1956 on Desolation Peak, which he recounts in *Lonesome Traveler*, *Desolation Angels*, and *The Dharma Bums*.

66

At Marblemount the [Skagit]
river is a swift torrent, the work
of quiet mountains… The air
smells of pine and sawdust and
bark and mud and twigs—birds
flash over the water looking
for secret fish.

99

Jack Kerouac, making his way to the North Cascades,
Lonesome Traveler (1960)

OLYMPIC
Port Angeles, Washington

Serving as a living laboratory for scientists, the park has four major ecosystems: subalpine, coast, temperate rainforest, and lowland forest.

The rainforest gets
144 inches (365 cm)
of water a year.

66

Bears have not killed
a single person in Olympic
National Park but a mountain
goat, which is not a native
species to the region, killed a
man in 2010.

99

New York Times, August 3, 2017

CHAPTER
FOUR

The Mountain West

From the Great Plains
to the Sierra Nevada,
this region is crossed by
the Rockies, the largest
mountain system in
North America.

GRAND CANYON
Grand Canyon, Arizona

The canyon is 10 miles (16 km) wide and 1 mile (1.6 km) deep, and reveals rock layers spanning time. The youngest layer is thought to be about 240 million years old, while the oldest rock is 1.7 billion years old.

The oldest human artifacts are nearly 12,000 years old.

There are
1,000 caves
hidden within the Grand Canyon.

Only 335 of those have been recorded and only one, the Cave of the Domes on the Horseshoe Mesa, is open to the public.

For the best viewpoints, visit Hopi Point off Hermit Road for watching sunset and sunrise or the Skywalk, managed by the Hualapai tribe and located on tribal lands, which is a horseshoe-shaped steel frame with a glass floor and sides that projects about 70 feet (21 meters) from the canyon rim.

"

Leave it as it is. You cannot improve on it. The ages have been at work on it, and man can only mar it.

"

President Theodore Roosevelt,
on the Grand Canyon, 1903

PETRIFIED FOREST
I-40 (Route 66), Arizona

With the largest concentrations of petrified wood in the world, at as much as 218 million years old, the Petrified Forest also has fossils that date to 225 million years old, from ferns and gingkoes to phytosaurs and dinosaurs.

The Painted Desert can
be accessed through the
north part of the forest and
continues into Navajo Nation.
Abundant iron and manganese
compounds give the rocks their
distinctive and vibrant red and
lavender colors.

SAGUARO
Tuscson, Arizona

Pronounced Sa-WAH-ro, the park is home to the nation's largest cacti. The slow-growing giant saguaro is a symbol of the American West and the oldest recorded was Old Granddaddy at 300 years old and 40 feet (12 meters) tall. The tallest was over 78 feet (23.8 meters).

Many signature reptile species are found in Saguaro National Park, including the venomous Gila monsters, desert tortoises, western coral snakes, six species of rattlesnake, and collared and desert spiny lizards.

BLACK CANYON OF THE GUNNISON
Montrose, Colorado

The gorge is so narrow and steep, dropping 240 feet per mile at Chasm View, that parts of it only receive 33 minutes of sunlight a day—a fact that gave it the name Black Canyon.

A narrow-gauge train once ran through the canyon, first for mining and then for carrying sheep and cattle for the thriving ranching industry. In 1949, the last train, a scenic excursion train, ran from Gunnison to Cimarron, and the depot, roundhouse, hotel, saloon, and residences all disappeared from the town.

"

We entered a gorge, remote
from the sun, where the rocks
were two thousand feet sheer,
and where a rock-splintered
river roared and howled ten feet
below a track which seemed
to have been built on the
simple principle of dropping
miscellaneous dirt into the

river and pinning a few rails a-top. There was a glory and a wonder and a mystery about the mad ride, which I felt keenly... until I had to offer prayers for the safety of the train.

"

Rudyard Kipling, on riding through the canyon in 1889

GREAT SAND DUNES
Mosca, Colorado

The tallest dunes in
North America, stretching
30 square miles (78 sq km),
are the centerpiece in a diverse
landscape of grasslands,
wetlands, forests, alpine lakes,
and tundra. The Star Dune rises
755 feet (230 meters)
from base to crest.

Sabkha mineral deposits can accumulate into thick crusts here. Early settlers collected the minerals to use in baking or laundry detergent and, in the 19th century, a tiny town appeared nearby called Soda City, where mineral blocks were manufactured and shipped out by train.

MESA VERDE
Cortez and Mancos, Colorado

The only national park
in the United States created to
protect cultural and historical
sites rather than natural
features, there are 4,000
archaeological sites and 600 cliff
dwellings in Mesa Verde, and
the park protects the heritage
of 26 tribes.

The elaborate stone communities on the mesas and cliffsides were built by the ancestral Pueblo people 1,400 years ago. The largest is Cliff Palace, with 150 rooms and 23 *kivas* (round rooms), which had a population of approximately 100 people.

ROCKY MOUNTAINS
Estes Park and
Grand Lake, Colorado

Acquired by the U.S. with
the 1803 Louisiana Purchase,
the Pike's Peak Gold Rush of
1859 drew hopeful miners and
speculators, as well as ranchers,
hunters, and homesteaders,
to the Rocky Mountains.

The range is 76 million years old and crosses 3,000 miles and six U.S. states. The high peaks and plains are still home to numerous indigenous people and here you will find reserves for the Bannock, Sioux, Blackfoot, Cow People, Apache, and Kutenai.

"

I have dropped into the very place I have been seeking, but in everything it exceeds all my dreams… The scenery is the most glorious I have ever seen, and is above us, around us, at every door.

"

Isabella Bird, English adventurer and the second woman to climb the Rockies, in *A Lady's Life in the Rocky Mountains* (1879)

A globally important bird
area, the park is home to
280 species of bird as well
as its unofficial mascot, the
bighorn sheep—some 400 of
these wander the park and
are known to be very gentle.

GLACIER
West Glacier, Montana

The park has pristine forests, alpine meadows, rugged mountains, and spectacular lakes, of which there are a whopping 700, but the active glaciers for which the park is named are rapidly disappearing, dropping from 150 in mid-1850s to 25 today.

Great Northern Railway, under the supervision of president Louis W. Hill, built a number of hotels and chalets throughout the park in the 1910s to promote tourism and portray it as "America's Switzerland."

CARLSBAD CAVERNS
Carlsbad, New Mexico

There are 119 known caves in the park, and the Big Room in Carlsbad Cavern, at

8.2 acres,

is the largest accessible cave chamber in North America.

The second deepest cave in
the continental U.S., only fully
discovered in 1986, Lechuguilla Cave
holds a variety of rare speleothems,
including gypsum chandeliers, hairs,
and beards, tubular "soda straws,"
cave pearls, and rusticles.

Rare bacterial strains, resistant to
antibiotics, have been found
in the cave. Unfortunately, or
perhaps fortunately, it is not open
to the public.

WHITE SANDS
Alamogordo, New Mexico

Glistening white sands over 275 miles, creating the world's largest gypsum crystal dunefield, arise from the Tularosa Basin, which has a rich cultural history of human occupation, from 10,000 years ago when ancient hunters stalked the local bison.

The sands, along with towering mountains, crystal-blue skies, stunning sunsets, and moonlit nights, make the park a popular movie and advertising location. Hollywood has filmed more than 20 major movies here since 1950, including the first two *Transformers* movies and numerous westerns, such as *Hang 'Em High* (1968), starring Clint Eastwood.

BIG BEND
Rio Grande, Texas

Historically, people traveled to the Hot Springs in Big Bend for healing.

Today, visitors can soak in the 105°F (40.5°C) water that gushes from the old foundation of a bathhouse, sited on the north bank of the Rio Grande.

Floating the Rio Grande River through Santa Elena Canyon is a popular activity but considered international travel— bring your passport!

GUADALUPE MOUNTAINS
Salt Flat, Texas

Part of the ancient horseshoe-shaped Capitan Reef that formed beneath a tropical ocean some 250 million ago, the mountains feature Guadalupe Peak, the highest point in the entire state of Texas at 8,749 feet (2,667 metres), as well as the massive promontory El Capitan, with an elevation of 8,078 feet (2,462 metres).

Watch out for reptiles in the Chihuahuan Desert!

There are snakes such as bullsnakes, coachwhips, and five different types of rattlesnake, the largest being the western diamondback.

ARCHES
Moab, Utah

Shaped by geological plate changes and water over 65 million years ago, this red rock wonderland rests on a salt bed and features over 2,000 natural stone arches and hundreds of soaring pinnacles, massive rock fins, and giant balanced rocks.

The natural stone arches are not permanent and are fragile, despite their rugged looks.

Even the world's most famous arch here, the magnificent Delicate Arch (also called Cowboy's Chaps, or Old Maid's Bloomers), will crumble and new ones form over time.

BRYCE CANYON
Bryce Canyon, Utah

The largest concentration
on earth of the distinctive
rock spires called hoodoos is
situated on top of the formation
called the Grand Staircase,
100 miles (161 km) of colorful
sedimentary rock layers that
reach from Bryce to the
Grand Canyon.

The story of Bryce Canyon, as related in 1936 by Indian Dick, a Paiute elder who then lived on the Kaibab Reservation, tells of the Legend people. Shape-shifting animals, birds, and lizards that looked like people but who were not, they were turned to rock ("red-painted faces") by the powerful Coyote spirit for their evil-doing.

CANYONLANDS
Moab, Utah

Carved by the Colorado and Green rivers, the rock formations here include a large mesa called the Island in the Sky, the colorful sandstone spires of the Needles, and the extremely remote and dangerous Maze, with features such as the Land of Standing Rock, the Wall, and Chocolate Drops.

A remote extension of
Canyonlands, Horseshoe Canyon
is known for its 200- foot
(61-meter)-long rock paintings of
supernatural and sinister figures,
some carrying weapons, a product
from the Desert Archaic culture,
a nomadic group of hunter-
gatherers. Human presence in the
canyon has been dated as far back
as 9,000–7,000 BCE.

CAPITOL REEF
Torrey, Utah

The park's Waterpocket Fold is a geologic monocline (a wrinkle on the earth) extending almost 100 miles (161 km), which created the distinctive features of red rock cliffs, canyons, bridges, and the white sandstone domes named after the Capitol building in Washington, D.C.

A small fruit-orchard settlement first called the Junction and then Fruita was founded here in 1800 by Latter-day Saints at the junction of Fremont River and Sulphur Creek.

As the village lacked a post office, mail was picked up at the Mail Tree, which can still be seen today.

ZION
Springdale, Utah

Meaning "a place of peace and relaxation" in Hebrew, the name was given to the area by the Mormons.

The cream, pink, and red sandstone cliffs were formed 250 million years ago and the water that drips from Weeping Rock in the canyon fell as rain over 1,000 years ago.

More than 1,000 plant species
are found in the park,
from graceful cottonwoods
and towering pines to prickly
pears, cholla, and yucca.
The hanging gardens support
beautifully colored shooting-
stars, monkeyflowers, and
columbines.

GRAND TETON
Moose, Wyoming

Ten miles south of Yellowstone, the Teton range is the youngest in the Rocky Mountains, beginning 6–9 million years ago, and rising almost straight up from Jackson Hole valley, with the highest peak at 13,770 feet (4,197 meters).

Some of the earliest settlers in
the 1800s were trappers trekking
west in search of beaver fur
for the top hats so popular at the
time. As fashions turned from
fur to silk hats, the era of
the mountain men faded away.

YELLOWSTONE
Wyoming

The oldest national park, Yellowstone is frequently referred to as the "American Serengetti" as every native large mammal survives here today, including bison, elk, mule deer, wolves, coyotes, pronghorn, black bears, grizzly bears, moose, mountain lions, bighorn sheep, and mountain goats.

66

Yellowstone is the only place in the U.S. where buffalo have roamed continuously since the prehistoric era. Numbering 5,000 strong, they make up the country's largest and oldest free-range herd.

99

National Geographic, March 22, 2019

Sited on an ancient volcanic caldera, the park contains the majority of all the geysers in the world.

Boardwalk trails provide easy access to some of the 10,000 hydrothermal features, which include hot springs, fumaroles, and mudpots.

Old Faithful,

the most famous geyser, erupts around 20 times a day.

Numerous Native Americans settled here, from Salish, Kiowa, Crow, and Sioux to contemporary Blackfeet, Cayuse, and Shoshone, and used the hydrothermal sites ceremonially and medicinally.

To the Kiowa, the Dragon's Mouth hot spring in the Mud Volcano area is where their creator bequeathed them the land for their ancestral home.

CHAPTER
FIVE

The Midwest

America's heartland and cowboy country, the terrain here stretches from the Badlands to the Great Lakes to the hot springs of Arkansas.

HOT SPRINGS
Hot Springs, Arkansas

The 47 hot springs here are the only nonvolcanic thermal springs in the U.S. The 8,000-feet (2,439-meter)-deep rock fractures that formed along with the Ouachita Mountains collect rainwater and heat it before the water hits a fault line and moves to the surface, a process that takes an astounding 4,400 years.

Known as the "American Spa,"
people have been coming here for
8,000 years for the therapeutic
waters, which have an average
temperature of 143°F (62°C) and
produce a million gallons a day.

The first bathhouses were
essentially brush huts and
log cabins placed over rock
excavations.

INDIANA DUNES
Porter, Indiana

Within easy reach of Chicago,
the park includes approximately
15 miles of Lake Michigan
shoreline and 50 miles of trails.
The sand dunes are habitat
to over 350 species of birds
and more than 1,100 flower
plants and ferns, including the
endangered fringed polygala,
or gaywing.

The sand is mostly quartz and silica left behind by glaciers and creates a unique sound when walked on, which gives the dunes the name "singing sands."

ISLE ROYALE
Houghton, Michigan

Acquired by the U.S. from Great Britain as part of the 1783 Treaty of Paris, this remote wilderness in the middle of Lake Superior is accessible only by ferry, seaplane, or private watercraft.

In addition to Isle Royale, the park encompasses up to 400 smaller islands, only 110 of which are named.

The most common large
mammals are moose and
gray wolves.

On the rare occasions when
Lake Superior completely
freezes over in winter, animals
from the mainland access
the island.

VOYAGEURS
International Falls, Kabetogama, Ash River, and Crane Lake, Minnesota

Four large lakes linked by smaller waterways make this park popular with canoeists, kayakers, other boaters, and fishermen as well as health seekers and vacationers.

By the time the park was established in 1975, over 60 resorts, 97 leased cabin sites, and 120 privately owned properties were located within the park's boundaries, including the spectacular summer homes of Rainy Lake.

The park is named for French Canadian voyageurs who paddled birchbark canoes for fur-trading companies in the late 18th and early 19th centuries. Famous for their boisterous songs and stamina, they could paddle up to 16 hours a day.

GATEWAY ARCH
St. Louis, Missouri

A memorial more than a park, the arch was built to honor St. Louis's and Thomas Jefferson's commitment to the nation's western expansion.

Designed by Eero Saarinen, it is the tallest structure in Missouri at 630 feet (192 meters) both tall and wide, with 1,076 steps in each "leg." Tram cars inside take visitors to the top viewing window.

Constructed to withstand strong winds, the arch can swing by as much as 18 inches (46 cm) in a 150-mph- (241-kph-) wind.

The arch can also withstand an

8.5 earthquake

on the Richter scale.

THEODORE ROOSEVELT
Medora, North Dakota

Teddy Roosevelt encountered the rugged landscape and wilderness lifestyle of the Little Missouri Badlands while hunting bison and ranching here as a young man. Experiencing the passing of one of the final frontiers of the West would shape his interest in parks conservation when he became president.

66

The Bad Lands grade all the
way from those that are almost
rolling in character to those
that are so fantastically broken
in form and so bizarre in color
as to seem hardly properly to
belong to this earth.

99

Theodore Roosevelt,
Hunting Trips of a Ranchman (1885)

BADLANDS
Southwestern South Dakota

The name Badlands comes from the Lakota Sioux tribe, who first called it *mako sica* or "the land that is bad," possibly because of the lack of water, difficult terrain, extreme temperatures, and clay soil that becomes slick and sticky in the rain.

One of the world's richest fossil beds, there is evidence of extinct animals and ancient horses and rhinos from 34–37 million years old, as well as alligators, saber-tooth cats, camels, and large and small rodents.

Clastic dikes, vertical sheets of rock that cross-cut horizontal layers of rock, hold up and secure the Badlands.

They are usually a different color than the surrounding rock, and the tan, green, and red colors are caused by minerals such as hematite (rust) and chlorite.

The park's stunning
panoramic landscape of
jagged pink-hued cliffs, buttes,
pinnacles, and spires became
internationally famous
after featuring in the film
Nomadland (2020).

WIND CAVE
Hot Springs, South Dakota

One of the longest, oldest, and most complex caves in the world, it is the third largest in the U.S. and the seventh largest in the world, with 143 miles of passages mapped to date.

Parts of the cave are over 300 million years old.

The maze of passages is home
to unique popcorn, frostwork,
and boxwork formations. Made
of thin blades of calcite that
project from cave walls and
ceilings, forming a honeycomb
pattern, boxwork is rarely found
anywhere else; in fact, 95% of
boxwork in the world is here.

CUYAHOGA VALLEY
Cleveland and Akron, Ohio

Cuyahoga is a Native American word meaning "crooked river," and the river, which feeds into Lake Erie, runs for 85 miles despite covering very little overall distance.

With 943 species of plants in the park, the most common are trees. Under tall oaks, maples, hickory, beech, pine, and spruce there are shorter understory trees such as American hornbeam and sassafras.

There are
100 waterfalls
here, the most popular
being the 60-foot- (18.2-meter-)
high Brandywine Falls,
the former site of saw, grist,
and woolen mills.

An 87-mile (140-km) towpath trail runs through the park, following the historic route of the Ohio & Erie Canal, built between 1825 and 1832.

CHAPTER
SIX

The South & North East

Covering two very diverse regions, here you will find caves and watery wonderlands in the southern states and the mountains and forests of Appalachia in the east.

BISCAYNE
Miami, Key Biscayne, and Homestead, Florida

The four ecosystems of Biscayne—shallow bay water, keys islands, reefs, and mangrove forest—lie between Key Biscayne and Key Largo. 95% of the park's nearly 173,000 acres are underwater.

More than 200 species of fish,
seabirds, whales, and hard
corals are here, including
16 endangered species, such
as the Schaus' swallowtail
butterflies, smalltooth sawfish,
manatees, and green and
hawksbill sea turtles.

Six shipwrecks have been mapped; the *Erl King* (sank 1891), *Alicia* (sank 1905), and *Lugano* (1913) are best for scuba diving, and the *Mandalay* (sank 1966) for snorkeling.

THREE LOST WRECKS

These wrecks are in the Biscayne waters but you won't find them on any chart.

♠ The British HMS *Fowey* warship (sank 1748) was launched from Hull, England, and identified in 1975.

♠ The "English China" wreck was a wooden sailing vessel about 65 feet (20 meters) long that may have caught fire and sunk. Carrying Staffordshire china, it could be the *Ledbury* (lost in 1769) or the *Hubbard* (lost in 1772), but the presence of Spanish-made *ladrillos* (bricks) cast doubt on its provenance.

♠ The "Soldier Key" wreck, a large, expensively built ship from the late 1700s to early 1800s, was carrying a cargo of Jamaican trade spice.

DRY TORTUGAS
Key West, Florida

Brilliantly clear open water with seven small islands and the 19th-century Fort Jefferson, the park is less than 1% dry land, and the corals and seagrass communities are among the most vibrant in all the Florida Keys.

Originally named *Las Tortugas* (Spanish for "the turtles") by Ponce de León in 1513 during his fabled quest for the elusive fountain of youth, the "dry" refers to the fact that there is no fresh water source. The abundance of sea turtles that annually nest in the area include the loggerhead, green turtle, hawksbill, leatherback, and Kemp's ridley.

It is illegal to disturb sea turtles and their nests.

Over 200 bird species migrate through the park each year and it's not uncommon to see 70 species in one day, including flamingos, warblers, nighthawks, owls, terns, falcons, pelicans, and cuckoos.

During a tropical storm, the writer Ernest Hemingway and a group of friends were stranded at Fort Jefferson for 17 days with only a short supply of canned goods, liquor, coffee, and the fish they caught from the ocean.

EVERGLADES
Miami, Naples, and Homestead, Florida

The park forms part of the Greater Everglades, the largest freshwater marsh in the U.S., which was coined the "River of Grass" by author and conservationist Marjory Stoneman Douglas. It is one of only three locations in the world to be listed as an international biosphere reserve, a World Heritage site, and a wetland of international importance.

The gladesmen culture is still alive today. Traditionally, they were men who built homes in the Everglades to hunt and fish in isolation. They navigated the narrow canals and waterways with small boats called "glade skiffs," and were deeply entrenched in the ecosystem.

"

Here are no lofty peaks seeking the sky, no mighty glaciers or rushing streams wearing away the uplifted land. Here is land, tranquil in its quiet beauty, serving not as the source of water, but as the last receiver of it. To its natural abundance we owe the spectacular plant and animal life that distinguishes this place from all others in the country.

"

President Harry S. Truman, Dedication of Everglades National Park, December 6, 1947

Created to protect a highly
endangered ecosystem, the
Everglades are an important
habitat for numerous rare and
endangered species like the
West Indian manatee, American
saltwater crocodile, wood
stork, snail kite, and the elusive
Florida panther.

MAMMOTH CAVE
Mammoth Cave, Kentucky

With 412 miles (663 km) of mapped passages, Mammoth is the world's longest cave system and named for the huge size of the cave's chambers and avenues (and not the prehistoric elephant-like mammal).

A treasure trove of fossils, including some from over 300 million years ago, the cave preserves Paleozoic bedrock and Cenozoic fossils.

Remains from animals that wandered, washed, or were dragged into the cave can also be found as fossils and include the hellbender, a large aquatic salamander, a giant short-faced bear, a mastodon, a saber-toothed cat, and, remarkably for the landlocked state, 40 species of shark.

ACADIA
Bar Harbor, Maine

The word Acadia is believed to derive from the native Mi'kmaq term *akadie* or *cadie*, meaning "a fertile land," and adapted to the French *L'Acadie*. The park features stunning coastlines of rocky beach, dense woodland, and glacier-scoured granite peaks such as Cadillac Mountain, the highest point on the East Coast.

Inhabited by Native Americans for 12,000 years, Acadia is the heartland of four distinct tribes—the Maliseet, Micmac, Passamaquoddy, and Penobscot—collectively called the Wabanaki, or People of the Dawnland.

GREAT SMOKY MOUNTAINS
North Carolina & Tennessee

The dramatic color change of foliage in the autumn helps make the Great Smokies America's most visited national park.

In 2020, 12.4 million people came to the park, despite closures due to the Covid-19 pandemic.

Variations in elevation, rainfall, temperature, and geology provide ideal habitat for over 1,600 species of flowering plants, including 100 native tree species and more than 100 native shrub species.

Another 450 species of non-flowering plants occupy the park, too.

Part of the homeland of
the Cherokee tribe, 13,000
members of the Eastern Band
of Cherokee live in the 56,000-
acre Qualla Boundary, the
Eastern gateway to the park.

"

If you drive to, say, Shenandoah National Park, or the Great Smoky Mountains, you'll get some appreciation for the scale and beauty of the outdoors. When you walk into it, then you see it in a completely different way. You discover it in a much slower, more majestic sort of way.

"

Bill Bryson, *A Walk in the Woods* (1997)

CONGAREE
Hopkins, South Carolina

A land of water and fire, the unique old-growth bottomland hardwood forest is regularly covered by floodwaters while the upland pine forest of fire-resistant trees rely on the wildfires to purge undergrowth and maintain the savannahs.

A lush floodplain forest, it has one of the highest deciduous canopies in the world and one of the largest concentrations of champion trees, such as the 167-foot (51-meter), 361-point loblolly pine.

VIRGIN ISLANDS
St. John, Virgin Islands

Prehistoric and archaeological sites date from as early as 840 BCE to the arrival of Columbus in 1493. Reef Bay petroglyphs carved by the Taino people into blue basalt rock around 500 CE on the edge of a pool are thought to be depictions of the faces and symbols of their ancestors and a way of communicating with the supernatural world.

Coral reefs, seagrass beds, and a 246-yard (225-meter) underwater snorkeling trail can be found at Trunk Bay in the Virgin Islands.

SHENANDOAH
Blue Ridge Mountains, near Luray, Virginia

The main feature of the park, the Blue Ridge Mountains, got their name from the color they display when seen from a distance. Trails run 500 miles (804 km) and include a 101-mile (161-km) section of the Appalachian Mountains, which were formed 300–500 million years ago.

Rapidan Camp, the summer retreat established by President and Mrs. Herbert Hoover during his administration in 1929, was the first complex specifically designed as a presidential retreat, and the precursor to Camp David (built in 1938.) The 13 buildings are connected by a network of paths and stone or wood bridges.

NEW RIVER GORGE
Hinton, Beckley, Glen Jean, and Fayetteville, West Virginia

The newest national park, designated in 2021, the park encompasses over 70,000 acres of land along 53 miles (85.3 km) of the New River from Bluestone Dam to Hawk's Nest Lake in the Appalachian Mountains.

A rugged whitewater river slicing through the mountains and flowing north through canyons, the New River is one of the oldest on earth, having had many names in the past, including the Cohnaway, the Wood, and even, by some tribes that lived in the area, the River of Death.

"

There can be nothing in the world
more beautiful than the Yosemite,
the groves of the giant sequoias
and redwoods, the Canyon of
the Colorado, the Canyon of the
Yellowstone, the Three Tetons; and
our people should see to it that they
are preserved for their children and
their children's children forever, with
their majestic beauty all unmarred.

"

President Theodore Roosevelt,
Outdoor Pastimes of an American Hunter **(1905)**